Helen Watkins.

Helen Watkins.

STUDIO VISTA

Portraits in Oils

JENNY RODWELL

STUDIO
VISTA

ACKNOWLEDGEMENTS

The author and publishers would like to thank the following
artists who have allowed us to use their work in this book:
Alastair Adams, pp. 10–11; Humphrey Bangham, pp. 8–9,
26–27; Antony Dufort, pp. 14–15; Brenda Holtam,
pp. 10–11; Jack Millar, pp. 6–7; Suzanne O'Riley, pp. 8–9,
48–49, 50–51; Norman Shawcross, pp. 6–7; Ian Sidaway,
pp. 4–5; Stan Smith, pp. 72–73; Alan Stones, pp. 12–13.
Special thanks to Winsor and Newton for their generous
help with materials; to Adrian Smith, Stan Smith and Aubrey
Wiseman for the artwork; to Humphrey Bangham, Suzanne
O'Riley, Ian Sidaway and Stan Smith for the step-by-step
demonstrations; and to Fred Munden for taking
the photographs.

Studio Vista
A Cassell imprint
Villiers House
41/47 Strand
London WC2N 5JE

First published 1994

British Library Cataloguing in Publication Data

A catalogue record for this book is available from the British Library

ISBN 0-289-80120-6

Series editors Jenny Rodwell and Patricia Monahan
The moral rights of the author have been asserted

Series designer Edward Pitcher

Distributed in the United States by
Sterling Publishing Co. Inc.
387 Park Avenue South, New York, NY 10016-8810

Typeset by Litho Link Ltd, Welshpool, Powys, Wales
Printed in Great Britain by Bath Colourbooks

CONTENTS

Introduction

M OST PEOPLE feel they can judge a portrait by one simple test: is it a likeness? The fear of this 'test', and the belief that there is some secret behind 'getting a likeness', prevent many from trying portrait painting for themselves. But there is no secret — it is a matter of careful preparation before you paint, and skill attained by practice and by the grasp of certain basic principles and techniques.

This book traces the vital preparatory steps, and introduces you to principles which will help you to paint what you see, rather than what you think should be there, so that the 'likeness' will come about of its own accord.

No two human faces are the same as each other; similarly, no two artists follow exactly the same procedures. Principles there may be, but there are no rigid rules in portrait painting — so for this book professional painters have undertaken projects which you can follow step by step, while the artists speak about their own individual ways of working.

The book is about oil painting. Oil is a forgiving and malleable medium, but thought and planning are still needed. The right subject — whether someone you know or a stranger — needs to be posed against a background, with thought given to composition and lighting. Preliminary drawings and sketches often help.

Double portrait *In an unusual version of the classical double portrait, Ian Sidaway's painting shows two workmen with the tools of their trade.*

THE LIVING FACE

The portrait once depicted not the living but the dead. The death mask allowed viewers to see the faces of those long gone, but in a way that was 'out of context' – with no background; just an isolated effigy with features frozen in what was usually a composed, expressionless manner.

The modern portrait artist, whether a painter or a photographer, confronts a much more complex set of problems. The faces are almost always those of the living; faces which need to convey feelings, mood and character. What is more, the people portrayed are not always set in isolation. Individuals are often positioned in environments which themselves have a story to tell.

The illustrations on this page show that there is no single way of painting a portrait. The approaches can be so varied that you have an enormous freedom of choice – but that same freedom calls for planning. There are questions to be answered even before setting up your easel. How can you best express the special qualities and characteristics of your subject? Do you want your portrait to be formal or informal? Will you paint just the head or do you prefer the whole figure? Will the figure be in a setting or do you want a plain background?

If you choose to place the portrait in an environment, make the setting positive. Suppose you decide to paint an individual in a domestic or work setting. In these cases, you would be painting not just a depiction of a person but an 'interior'. The Dutch painters of the sixteenth and seventeenth centuries mastered this approach brilliantly. Their subjects are actively interwoven with their settings: they play their musical instruments in furnished corners by open windows; they pour from earthenware pitchers in working kitchens.

There is another way in which the subject is integrated into the environment. Some artists make it quite clear that the subject is inside his or her home – an intimate touch is added.

The isolated subject
Sometimes, however, the artist wants the face or figure to say it all, without background. One approach can be to set the figure against a plain wall that does not distract. But even in this case the wall usually has tone and texture, indicating that space exists between the figure and its background. Thus the figure is in three-dimensional space.

Alternatively, the environment can be removed

altogether, as in the painting on this page by Norman Shawcross, who paints his subject against the stark whiteness of the primed canvas.

Portraiture as a record

Perhaps more than any other artist, the portrait painter has played the historic role of official recorder. Just as we catch a glimpse of the past by reading a biography, so we can look back through the centuries by viewing people who have been preserved in portrait, not as dead masks but as living characters.

In the fifteenth century, for instance, the Dutch artist Jan van Eyck (d. 1441) was the equivalent of an official photographer or witness at the betrothal of the man and woman portrayed in the famous 'Arnolfini Wedding'. The painting is vivid evidence that the event took place.

△ **The important setting** *In some compositions the setting is as important as the subject. 'Interior Evening' by Jack Millar shows how a figure can be the focal point yet occupy only a small part of the picture.*

▷ **Minimal background** *In his portrait of writer Francis Stuart, Norman Shawcross leaves the background as flat white, without attempting to create an illusion of three-dimensional space.*

THE GOOD LIKENESS

Portrait painters often face an awesome moment of truth: is it a 'good likeness'? This is one of the most difficult areas of portrait work, but there are guidelines which help to overcome the problems.

Instant attraction to detail can be a trap. The beginner may fret because the 'eyes are wrong' and consequently spend far too much time on this feature alone. The result could be that the eyes stand out from the rest of the face, often with overbright whites and a glassy stare.

An experienced artist, on the other hand, sees the eyes in relation to the other features and to the face as a whole. No single feature is more developed than another, and the whole face is kept in a state of flux until all the relationships are correctly established. Look closely at the majority of portrait paintings and you will see that the eyes are often no more than perfectly placed flicks of paint.

The human face is made up of different features — eyes, nose, chin, mouth and so on. As single elements they are far less important than you might think. What matters much more is how the features relate to each other.

The likeness, therefore, is not a mysterious ingredient. If you get the basic proportions and drawing right, then the painting will look like the sitter. It is a test of observation and accurate drawing rather than a special gift of vision. Quite simply, a good portrait is a good painting.

Character and gesture

Artists differ over whether it is a good idea to 'know your subject'. Many find it helpful to paint a sitter they know. Not only are they familiar with the face but they are also more relaxed with the subject. The 'Artist's Father' is one of several studies done of his parents by Humphrey Bangham.

Other artists prefer to paint a stranger. An unknown sitter helps them to take a fresh look at the subject. The painter then begins work free of any preconceptions.

◁ **The familiar face** *Artist Humphrey Bangham is most at home when painting faces he knows well. This portait of his father is one of several studies of the same subject.*

TETL
4 weeks

—20 oct
Dawn Pearson
02/61

556963

◁ ◁ **Movement and gesture** '*Young Man Smoking' by Suzanne O'Riley captures a fleeting moment as the subject raises a cigarette to his lips.*

Sometimes a person is characterized – recognized – more by his or her gestures than by any physical feature – a typical tilt of the head, an expression, a certain way of sitting. Look carefully for the clues.

In the painting on this page of the young man smoking, the likeness has more to do with characteristic movements and facial expressions as he lights a cigarette than with physical likeness.

So, even when painting a stranger, spend a few minutes chatting before you freeze your model into a pose. This will give you the chance to observe your subject moving and talking. Informal drawings and quick sketches before painting will also allow you to weigh up your subject.

CONTEXT

The velvet and lace of some historical portraits offer obvious clues about the subject – showing their wealth and often their rank. But clothing plays another, purely pictorial, role as well. It adds texture, tone and colour to the painting as a whole. This is particularly the case nowadays, when easily available fabrics say less about economic and social status but nevertheless give the artist plenty of visual scope.

Thus, although the face tells us a lot about the character of the subject, the rest of the painting can often reveal much more.

The conversation piece

This is the term for a genre in which two or more people are usually depicted seated or posed inform-ally, often husband and wife or other family members, against the setting of their own home, gardens or grounds.

Here, the setting gives sitters an instant identity – a peep into their lives. Good examples, which also fascinate historians, are the conversation pieces of the eighteenth century, such as those by the English artists Thomas Gainsborough (1727–88) and William Hogarth (1697–1764).

The modern equivalent of a conversation piece would include a subject or subjects in their place of work – office, studio or building site. The workmen with their barrow and tools on pages 4–5 and this

◁ **Groups** *This study of commuters on the Underground by Brenda Holtam is a rapid colour sketch of people who were not aware they were being painted.*

△ **Places of work** *'Oddbins' by Alastair Adams. The artist finds that the workplace is often more unusual and visually stimulating than a domestic setting.*

woman in her wine-shop workplace are good examples.

Double portraits and groups

When painting two or more people in the same portrait, it is even more important to develop the painting as a whole. Don't treat the work as two separate portraits which happen to be on the same canvas. There may be two subjects, but visually you are painting the same image, so treat the composition as an integrated whole, making the colours, tones and textures work together across the whole of the painting.

The formal and informal

Artists talk of two distinct categories of portrait –

the formal and the informal. One of the differences between them is that in the former the subject generally looks directly at the artist or poses especially for the picture. He or she is obviously aware of the artist.

When the subject's attention is not focused on the artist, then a certain tension is released which makes for a more relaxed, informal portrait. In double and group portraits, the attention of the sitters may be focused on each other. There are tensions here, but they are different ones. They lie between the sitters themselves, perhaps, as they look at each other; or their attention may be held elsewhere as they look at something either in or out of the picture.

In the painting by Brenda Holtam, the subjects are travellers on the Underground and are seemingly unaware of the artist. Conversely, the painting of the workmen is obviously posed. The subjects are posing specifically for the portrait and both are looking directly at the artist.

11

THE SELF-PORTRAIT

Look around any art gallery, and look at the portrait examples in this book. There is no single, correct way of painting a portrait. Artists develop their own approaches through trial and error, and often through looking at the work of others.

One of the great drawbacks of portrait painting is that the artist is often restricted by the need to please. This is particularly the case with professional portrait artists, who are usually commissioned on the basis of previous results. They become typecast into working in a particular way, and development and experiment become impossible.

To offset this, painting your own portrait provides the perfect opportunity for trying out new approaches and different techniques. With yourself as the sitter, you are not obliged to struggle with a tight or representational painting, and there is no one to please except yourself. For the beginner, this is probably the best and most accessible way of learning how to paint portraits.

Stepping outside ourselves

Whatever its advantages, the self-portrait does present certain problems. For a start, we all have a self-image. We think of ourselves in a particular way, which often has nothing to do with how others see us. This is why, when we look in the mirror, we adopt a certain expression.

When painting yourself, therefore, you should try to be honest – to adopt the honesty of work which comes more easily when painting a complete stranger. You must be able to step outside yourself and overcome the utter familiarity of your own face sufficiently to make acccurate and objective visual statements. (Possibly this why so many great portraits have a particularly intense or haunting look.)

The Dutch painter Rembrandt (1609–69) painted himself at various stages throughout his life, documenting his progress from confident, successful young artist to disillusioned and poor old man. The portraits reflect the rise and fall of his fortunes and popularity.

In a similar way, the self-portraits shown here are from a series by contemporary painter Alan Stones. Again, the images are a personal record – in this case of troubled and then eventually happier times in the artist's life.

△ **Setting up** *Artist Alan Stones at work on one of his self-portraits. The positioning of the easel, mirror and light source is all-important. Allow enough space to enable you to stand back from the work and assess progress.*

Two of a series of self-portraits painted by Alan Stones over a period of two years.

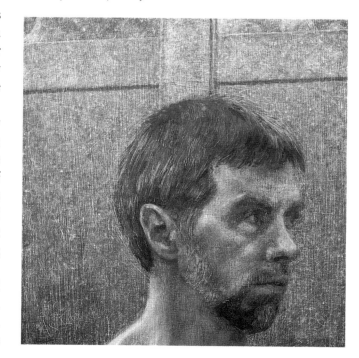

Thinking ahead

E VEN IF your portrait consists of only a head and shoulders against a plain background, the background and composition need careful planning. Where will the subject be positioned and how will you deal with the surrounding shapes?

There is an unlimited choice of backgrounds, both outdoors and in your home or studio. But perhaps the most satisfying is the one you create yourself, building it up so that the background arrangement takes on its own life.

The French artist Edouard Vuillard (1868–1940) took enormous delight in pattern and decoration. His figures almost always appear before a cacophony of wallpapers, printed fabrics, woven designs and any other manufactured material. It is a good idea to keep a selection of old curtains, bedspreads – anything giving a choice of colour or pattern.

To help you think about background and composition, follow the well-tried technique of cutting a rectangular shape out of a sheet of paper or card and viewing your subject through the frame. Move the frame in much the same way as a photographer moves a camera in order to find the best shot. Alternatively, cut two L-shaped brackets which can be moved around and adjusted to form a rectangle of any proportion.

The figure sits alone in an empty room, giving a sense of space and solitude to this portrait. Antony Dufort painted the picture from life with the help of preliminary drawings.

BACKGROUNDS

The background is not an afterthought. Too many beginners plunge straight into an attempt to capture the features of a sitter before even thinking about the composition as a whole. Plan the background as part of the picture. This may involve arranging a special background or moving the sitter to a different location.

To professional portrait painters, choice of background can be critical. Sitters, too, often have strong ideas about this, and many want to be portrayed in a setting of personal significance – perhaps the workplace or a special room in the home.

These factors can extend the portrait into a more complex and interesting work. Often, they call for as much attention to be paid to the background as to the person being painted. The portrait becomes an interior with other elements, such as artefacts and furniture, which must be arranged and incorporated into the composition.

The alternative to a busy background is to opt for a minimal or plain backdrop to ensure that the surroundings do not dominate the main subject. Even this should be planned in advance, though, because it will still play a vital role in the finished painting.

Plain backgrounds

A sense of space is important in all paintings. If your portrait is painted realistically, in three-dimensional terms, with light and shade to describe the form, then an illusion of space has already been

▽ *The background affects how we perceive a subject. Busy backgrounds can confuse the image, unless the background colour is unrelated to the colours on the subject. Warm backgrounds bring out the warm flesh tones; a cool background emphasizes cooler tones. A light background shows up the shape of a darker figure; a darker background blends with dark tones on the subject.*

Dark background

Light background

Warm background

created on the canvas. A flat background can contradict this visual illusion, which is why backgrounds are rarely painted as completely flat colours, even when the sitter is portrayed against a plain, featureless wall.

A background wall is almost always uneven, particularly when the subject is lit from the side, causing the part of the wall closest to the light source to be lighter in tone. Thus the painting of a flat wall will usually be graduated – going from light to dark behind the figure.

Tone and colour

Whatever background colour you choose, that colour will be picked up and emphasized elsewhere in the painting. This is particularly relevant with portraits, because flesh tones of all races tend to contain a normally unnoticed mixture of colours, ranging from warm pinks, browns and yellows to cool blues and greens. Thus a cool background will pick up cool shadow tones, giving the whole painting an overall coolness. A warm background tends to emphasize the pinks and yellows of the flesh, giving the portrait an overall warmth.

The paintings in this book show that artists normally choose to illuminate the sitter with a strong side light. This is a classical portrait-painting technique, popular because it shows the form of the face clearly in well-defined planes of light and shade. Thus lit, however, one side of the face is strongly illuminated while the other is in equally strong shade. This makes the background tone particularly important. With a light background, the illuminated side of the face often merges with the background; against a dark background, the same thing can happen to the shaded side of the face.

The side-light approach is fine, provided it produces the desired effect. The demonstration painting on page 59, for instance, is deliberately set up in this way because the artist chose to soften the contour on one side of the subject's face. However, if you want the head as a whole to stand out from the background, then you must select a medium-toned background, or one that provides enough contrast for the subject to stand out clearly.

Cool background

Busy background, intrusive colour

Busy background, contrasting colour 17

THE RIGHT POSE

It is important that your sitter is comfortable from the start. A natural position will look and feel right and will be easier to hold for a long time. An awkward pose, as well being difficult to maintain, will be reflected in the painting. Try several different poses, asking your sitter which feel right and which don't.

Normally a portrait subject will be seated. This means he or she can keep the pose for relatively long periods. With a standing pose, remember to allow for frequent rests for the subject. Professional artists' models take a fifteen-minute break every forty-five minutes – more if they are holding a difficult pose. Don't get so carried away with your painting that you completely forget the needs of the sitter. If necessary, ask your subject to tell you when it's time for a rest.

Angles of the head

In many portraits, the composition consists quite simply of a full-frontal view, with the subject looking directly at the artist. This approach works well for many painters, particularly when the artist is interested primarily in the character of the sitter, rather than in the background and the surroundings. For the beginner, the full-frontal might seem attractive because it sounds easy – but this is not necessarily the case.

The nose, eye sockets and underlying structures are less prominent when you are looking at the face from the front; the forms of the features can be seen less clearly. There really is a three-dimensional structure to the full-frontal face, yet the inexperienced do not look for this. Instead, they tend to fall back on preconceived ideas of what they know should be there, rather than looking at what they can actually see. The result might well be a squashed nose, staring eyes and a pancake face, similar to the pictures done by children.

Do not let this difficulty put you off the full-frontal view. Just don't presume that it is necessarily

the easiest to paint. As an alternative, however, you can paint your subject in profile, presenting an absolute side view of the face – especially effective if the subject has prominent or distinctive features.

A more natural view lies half-way between a profile and a full-front view and is sometimes referred to as a three-quarters view.

Marking the pose

Finding exactly the same pose after a break can be tricky. You will find it helpful if you mark the sitter's position with chalk or strips of masking tape so that he or she can easily get back into the same pose. For a painting which takes several sittings, mark the position of the chair legs as well.

Inevitably, sitters relax during a long session, so it is wise to give your subject a few minutes to settle down after each break before starting to paint. It is also a good idea to get your sitter to fix his or her eyes on a constant point – this way the angle and direction of the head will remain constant.

Fabrics are more problematic, for you will never get pleats and folds in clothing to fall in exactly the same place twice. Perhaps the best approach is to keep clothes and drapes in a sketchy, fluid state in the picture until the final stages. Another approach is to paint the clothes as they first appear and then ignore any subsequent changes.

Two classical portrait poses are profile (far left) and full-frontal (left).

A three-quarter view (right) combines the advantages of the profile and full-frontal view.

LIGHTING

So you pose your sitter and arrange the background, and begin the painting . . .

At first, everything is fine, but after a while the subject begins to change before your very eyes. Shadows appear, highlights that had not been so noticeable. Tones and colours seem to have changed.

You forgot to think about the lighting.

The effects of natural light are notoriously inconsistent, changing not only with the time of day but also with the weather conditions, which can alter radically from minute to minute. Yet, despite this – and despite the need for a constant light source to illuminate the subtle colours and forms of the human face – most artists prefer natural light. It is softer and does not distort colour.

If you choose to work by natural light, a north-facing one is undoubtedly the best, because it is more constant and does not cast heavy, changing shadows across the subject's face. Light from other directions, particularly the south, is subject to harsher shadows and starker contrasts.

In an ideal world you would paint at similar times of day and at similar stages in the weather. In the real world, you should be aware of the problem, establish a plan for colour and tone and stick to it. Sketches and photographs can be helpful here.

Daylight substitutes

Ordinary artificial light bulbs are less sympathetic than natural daylight and distort the colours on the subject. More seriously, they also distort the colours laid out on the palette, sometimes making it difficult to see the difference between one tube of colour and another, let alone to differentiate between the more subtle and similarly toned flesh colours.

One solution for the portrait painter is to use daylight bulbs. These are not identical to natural lighting, but they are a reasonable substitute and have the advantage of consistency. You can use daylight bulbs instead of natural lighting or you can install bulbs by a window and use them to replace the daylight as it fades or changes.

△ *The subject is lit from behind, obscuring the features in dense shadow and making the face too dark to paint.*

△ *A white screen, placed on the nearside of the subject, provides a soft reflected light which shows up the features.*

Direct or diffuse light

A strong directional light produces emphatic areas of light and shade. Some artists like the dramatic effects of chiaroscuro, as these exaggerated shadow and highlight patterns are called, because the features and underlying muscle structure of the subject are so clearly defined. Typically, chiaroscuro paintings show the subject against a dark background, with bright highlights where certain features catch the directional light.

If you find a directional light source is too strong,

Front lighting

Side lighting

Top lighting

the effects can be softened by placing a white sheet or gauze across the offending window or lamp. Alternatively, you can soften the shadows on the face by placing a white screen or sheet on the shaded side of the subject. This can be adjusted to produce a soft, reflected glow on the dark side of the face.

A broad overhead light would enable you to follow the example of Leonardo da Vinci (1452–1519) and light your subject from above. Leonardo did this to re-create as closely as possible the effects of natural sunlight, because that is how we normally perceive people and it therefore allowed him to get a better likeness of the sitter. He argued that if you met a close friend who was illuminated from below, the face would look so unfamiliar that you would probably not recognize it.

Lighting is one of the most important factors in portrait painting, so it is well worth spending some time discovering the possibilities. It is a mistake simply to sit your subject on the nearest chair and start painting. If you can't move your source of light, try moving the subject and see what a difference this can make.

COMPOSITION

Even if your portrait is a full-frontal view of a head and shoulders against the simplest background, you should still consider the composition. Too much empty space around the figure can make the painting look sloppy and unstructured. Too little space and the figure appears squashed and cramped.

The background has 'shape'; it is not just leftover space. So you should treat this positively and establish the areas of background as shapes in their own right. And it is not only shape; the background also consists of tone, colour and texture, all of which have a bearing on the actual subject.

Scale and proportion

A portrait is not necessarily small. It can be as big as you like, especially if you want to include most of the figure and a lot of background as well. Keep an open mind about the scale of your picture. Eventually, you may decide that a particular size suits you best, but initially you would do well to experiment and explore different possibilities.

Normally we think of a portrait as being vertical rather than horizontal. The figure or human head fits conveniently into a vertical rectangle, which is why it is often referred to as a 'portrait' shape. Used horizontally, the same rectangle is called 'landscape'.

Again, we should not make assumptions but should consider every possibility before automatically starting to paint on the good old 'portrait' rectangle. It sometimes make a refreshing change to see a portrait treated in an unusual way, perhaps on a horizontal rectangle, with the figure offset to one side; or perhaps on an exaggeratedly tall rectangle, as the artist has done with her painting on page 8.

The illustrations here show a few of the many different ways in which a typical portrait subject can be planned and painted.

Space and harmony

The object of most compositions is to create a harmonious balance of shapes and colours and to avoid any discordant or uncomfortable element in the picture.

Portraits are naturally harmonious in that the human face is an automatic focal point, and the viewer's eye is immediately attracted to that point. Even so, bad planning and clumsy handling can destroy this natural advantage. It is possible, for example, to put a figure too close to the edge of the support. This is especially damaging if the subject is looking outwards, past the frame, because the viewer's eye, and interest, are then led out of the picture. A clumsily positioned hand or arm can have a similarly discordant effect.

Portraits containing more than one figure are generally arranged so that the subjects have equal importance in the picture, but not in every case. With two or more sitters, there is greater scope for composing the subject within the canvas area, and you should aim to make the subjects complement each other without imposing a rigid symmetry on the painting.

The model sits on a garden seat against a wide background of flowers, foliage and stonework. Before starting to paint, the artist views the subject through two L-shaped brackets, moving these around to find suitable compositions for a portrait painting.

A whole range of expressions shows just how much a change of mood can alter the human face.

THE HUMAN FACE

We have seen most of our friends and acquaintances in different moods – smiling, pensive, relaxed, agitated and so on. We come to recognize them in these moods, and the recognition is so automatic that we tend not to notice the dramatic facial changes that each change of mood brings.

A change of expression is a structural change. As the underlying facial muscles contract or relax, they completely alter the contours and surface forms of the face. It is important, therefore, to consider the facial expression of the sitter before we start painting.

It is not just a question of whether the finished portrait makes the subject appear happy or sad. The expression is important in another way, one which is often ignored – the simple matter of how possible it will be for the subject to maintain a particular facial expression throughout several sittings.

Keep it general

We have said there is nothing mysterious about the ability to get a good likeness. Obviously the likeness is important, especially when the sitter is usually

there for that very reason. But it should not become an obsession. Although it is difficult to do this, try to forget you are painting a person. Try instead to see your subject as an arrangement of forms, shapes, colours and tones. Get these right and the likeness will take care of itself.

It is the correct relationship of one element to another that creates an accurate likeness. Remember, the spaces between the features are as important as the features themselves. It is no good painting the perfect nose if the nose is in the wrong place.

Remember that it is a great mistake in portrait painting to pay too much attention to detail. The problem is that when a certain part of the face has been painted in great detail, it requires enormous willpower to change it should it prove to be wrong.

One very good way of avoiding the temptation to overdo the detail is to use large brushes. In this way, you are forced to concentrate on the overall image, and it becomes easier to keep the painting in a state of flux and change.

It is important to avoid the abnormal stare that often results when inexperienced portrait painters overestimate the importance of eyes. Eyes may be the natural focal point of the face, but they should not be painted in more detail than the rest of the face. The commonest mistake is to make the whites of the eyes too bright. Take particular care to relate the whites of the eyes to the surrounding tones; they are usually darker than you think.

25

Basic anatomy

Y OU DON'T have to spell or pronounce sternocleido-mastoids to be a portrait painter, but it helps to be aware of them. They are part of the structure of the head and shoulders, and it is important to the artist to know a little anatomy.

Medical knowledge is unnecessary, but it is best to adopt a logical approach when you are drawing and painting, so that you understand how surface changes in the face and torso are caused by muscular movements under the skin.

For instance, the portrait artist takes note of how the head is attached to the neck, and how the movement of the neck affects that of the head. This action is caused by two muscles which pass from behind each ear to the breastbone: the sternocleidomastoid muscles. If you can be aware of their presence and what they do, then your portrait will be the more convincingly structured and therefore more realistic and naturalistic.

In an infant's face, the eye sockets are disproportionately large. A child's jawbone is underdeveloped and the features tend to be in the lower part of the face. The growth of teeth makes the jaw more prominent, lengthening the face. Adult bones usually keep their shape but, as cartilage changes and teeth are sometimes lost, there is an apparent shrinkage of the head in old age.

Preliminary drawing *The facial proportions of babies and young children differ from those of adults. Humphrey Bangham used coloured pencil for this exploratory drawing of one of his children.*

HEAD AND FACE

It is now time to pause for a brief excursion into anatomy, to take a look at what happens under the skin. We know that facial expressions make a considerable difference to the portait – that you cannot make a person smile simply by turning up the corners of the mouth, or make the same person look sad merely by making the mouth turn down. Such expressions are caused by muscular movements which affect the whole face, so to paint a convincing expression means knowing a little about the muscles themselves.

The head

The skull is made up of two basic parts – the cranium and the jaws. The cranium, which encloses the brain, dictates the shape of the head. It varies considerably from person to person, and can be an important and distinctive part of a portrait. It is useful to establish the shape of the cranium correctly in the early stages of the portrait, because other features can then be positioned correctly in relation to this. A thick head of hair can obscure this shape, but the hair itself is dictated by the bony shape underneath.

The cranium of a young baby is larger in relation to the face than that of adults.

The muscles

Muscles in the face are used in order to speak, eat, blink and sniff. In other words, they are connected to the facial orifices – the mouth, the eyes and the nose.

▷ *The rounded surface forms of the human face make it hard to differentiate between light and shaded areas because the two merge gradually on the rounded surface. Here, the artist has ignored the 'roundness' in order to establish the forms in visible planes of light and shade.*

The muscles around the mouth are particularly significant. They form the lower part of the face, and are the 'mound' which causes the mouth and lips to stand proud of the facial structure. The lips are not just a flat shape painted on to a flat face. They are part of an arrangement of forms which make up the lower half of the face.

Similarly, the top of the face is dominated by the eye sockets and the muscles which open and close the eyes. Some of these muscles surround the eye cavities; others join the brow of the eye to the forehead and scalp. The visible parts of the eyeballs are relatively small and can be painted only in the context of the bone-and-muscle structure which contains them.

Facial 'planes'

For the artist, it is not particularly helpful to know the names of the various muscles, but it is essential to know that they are there and to be able to see how the internal structure affects the external features.

The painter sees muscles as forms covered by flesh. These are made visible as the light catches the face, showing up the 'planes' – the highlights and shadows, and patches of warm and cool skin colour. These are the parts which together form the whole: the sitter's face.

The best way to understand the concept of planes is to imagine an origami ball – a paper structure which, instead of having a continuous, rounded surface, is made up of tiny, regular, flat surfaces. These surfaces are known as planes and each catches the light in a different way.

In a similar way, the human face can be observed as a series of planes – not regular, like those on the origami ball, but corresponding in shape and size to the bones and muscles underneath. In the illustration here, the artist has used oil paint to pick out the facial planes in observed warm and cool flesh tones.

◁ *A three-quarters view is asymmetrical. One side of the face is further away, and the artist must bear in mind that all the facial planes recede slightly.*

HANDS

Hands and arms are rivals to the face, drawing attention away from it. If you want to include hands in your portrait, they must be painted and positioned with care; the hands and arms inevitably become an important part of the composition.

Because they are more or less the same colour and tone as the face, hands and face are perceived simultaneously. This can be turned to your advantage, and you can use the similar tones to create a harmonious balance in the composition. But if the hands are clumsily positioned or badly painted, they will create discord and become an unwelcome focal point.

Composing the hands
Clasped hands are perhaps the most used compositional device in portraits. In such paintings, the arms form an enclosed shape, with the head at the top and the clasped hands at the bottom. This arrangement is usually comfortable to look at, but the composition can appear very symmetrical, especially when the clasped hands and the face-form are the same size and a similar shape. Avoid this symmetry by offsetting the figure, or at least offsetting the hands so they do not fall directly under the face.

A similar rule applies when the hands are positioned separately – perhaps laid on the sitter's knees or resting on a desk or table. Here, too, the composition can be very dull and symmetrical, with the hands forming the base of a regular triangle. One solution is to avoid having both hands on the same level.

It is always a mistake to allow fingers, hands or bare arms to go off the bottom of the picture. This cut-off point becomes an immediate focus, and the viewer's attention will be drawn towards the bottom edge of the picture when it should be resting on the face and figure.

Drawing and painting hands
Hands are much simpler to draw or paint than might at first appear. Difficulties arise only when artists try to paint each finger separately, without seeing the fingers and thumbs in the context of the rest of the hand.

Clasped hands, hands on knees and hands holding a book – common positions for the hands in many portraits. When drawing these hands, the artist started by making light construction lines showing the main planes and directions.

Hands can and should be simplified. Whether you are looking at a clenched fist, an open palm or a relaxed, drooping hand, it is a good idea to start with some basic construction lines. If you can first establish the planes across the hand, knuckles and wrist, as the artist has done in the illustrations here, then the underlying structure of the hand will be sound, and the fingers can be integrated into this.

We often see portraits in which the hands have been suggested – roughly sketched and blocked in – instead of being painted in the same detail as the rest of the painting. Sometimes, the hands are no more than a series of well-placed brush-strokes. Usually, the reason is that the artist wants to establish the hands without distracting attention from the face.

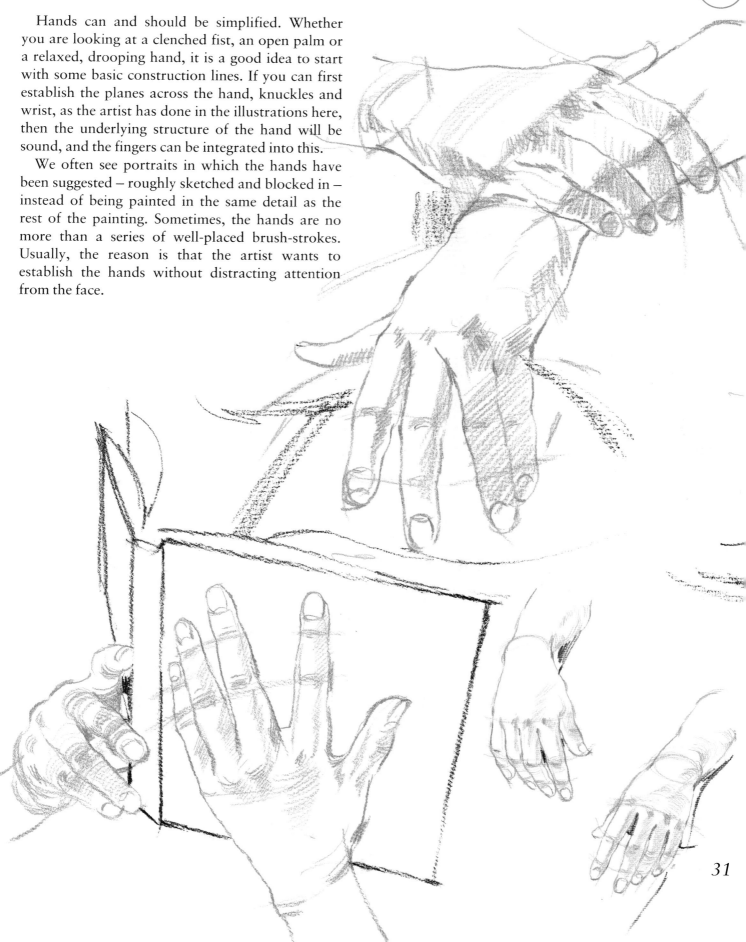

FLESH TONES

Have no preconceptions about the colour of skin. Once you look very closely at the skin tones of the subject, you will realize how hugely the colours can change from one part of the face to another. Some of these variations are changes in the local colour within the face – a red nose or pink cheeks, for instance. But by far the greatest reason for colour changes is that skin picks up and reflects surrounding colours, and can also look completely different depending on whether it is in the light or the shade.

The local colour of the skin affects the tones, but does not greatly influence the range of cools and warms, or the colours we choose for the palette. With both light-skinned and dark-skinned people, the local colour determines the basic tones to some degree, but the direction and strength of lighting are what really create the final colour variations. Black skin is more affected by reflected light than white skin, but in each case it is the relationship between the light and dark areas that is important to the painter.

Colour temperature
Highlights and shadows are never simply a lighter or darker version of the same general skin tone. Each has its own colour temperature, and you will see that shadows contain more grey, blue, green and cool purples, whereas lighter areas generally contain more warm browns, yellows, reds and oranges.

Approaches to painting flesh differ considerably. In the Renaissance, it was common to underpaint the flesh areas with a mixture of terre-verte and lead white. The cool green underpainting, showing through the warmer skin tones, gave the subjects a rather ethereal look.

Modern and contemporary artists still use glazing techniques similar to those employed by Renaissance

▷ **Warm tones** *Some random light skin colours mixed from white, Indian red, cadmium yellow and alizarin crimson.*

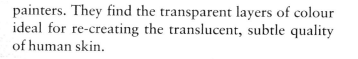

painters. They find the transparent layers of colour ideal for re-creating the translucent, subtle quality of human skin.

Choosing a palette

Choice of colour is a personal one, and most artists develop their own palette after considerable trial and error. The artists who produced the demonstration paintings worked in colours of their own choice. As a rule, the palette was the artist's standard one, with the quantity of colours adapted to suit the subject.

Although the overall palette differed from artist to artist, certain colours were used by all of them when painting the flesh tones. The common colours were yellow ochre, raw umber, white and a brownish red – either burnt sienna, Indian red or Venetian red. Each artist also used at least one blue and a strong, light yellow.

With experience, you will develop your own choice of colours, and for the step-by-step demonstrations you will need the colours used by the artist. As a general guide, however, you do not need a vast range of colours. In fact, initially you would be wise to stick to a limited one, adding to it as you feel the need to experiment and expand your repertoire.

The following colours will give you a basic palette and are perfectly adequate for the newcomer to portrait painting: white, black, cadmium red, alizarin crimson, cadmium yellow, yellow ochre, ultramarine, burnt sienna, raw sienna, burnt umber and viridian. Additional colours used by artists in the step-by-step projects are cerulean blue, manganese blue, Prussian blue, Naples yellow, Venetian red, flesh tint, Payne's grey and vermilion.

◁ **Cool tones** *Shadow colours achieved by adding small amounts of cobalt blue, viridian green or Payne's grey to the warmer tones.*

Materials and equipment

W HETHER USING a studio or a room at home, attention to certain basics will make your painting easier and more successful: storage, comfort for you and the sitters (see page 18), position of the easel for minimum disturbance and lighting (see page 20).

If you cannot find a permanent workroom, a mobile set of shelves is valuable, preferably with 'open storage' so you can see brushes, paints, cleaning materials and rags. Professionals often use plan chests, with wide, flat drawers.

For storing completed oil paintings, it easy to make an open rack in which the canvases can stand upright and separate. In this way they are easily accessible while taking up minimum space.

As oil paint gets old it forms a dry skin. This means that if you leave oils on your palette without cleaning them off, the old paint will turn brittle and can flake into pieces and interfere with any new paints squeezed on top. There is a second reason to clean your palette at the end of each painting session: a fresh palette gives you pure colours and a clean surface on which to mix them; this will be reflected in the colours of your final picture.

Pigments *Oil paints are made from pigments mixed with an oil binder. Some pigments are natural and come from earth, vegetable and even animal sources. Others, including the cadmiums and cobalts, come from metal salts. The first oil painters ground and mixed their own paints from pigments that varied both in quality and in colour. Modern oil paints are tested to ensure consistency.*

35

PAINTS

The artists who contributed to this book were unanimously of the opinion that one of the most important factors is to buy a reliable brand. Each had experience of making false economies, of choosing bargain brands only to discover that they were made either of poor pigment or with an excess of oil.

The best paints are artists' quality made to the highest possible standards and from the finest pigments. These are relatively expensive, although the pigment strength of quality paints makes them economical in the sense that they go much further than the less expensive brands.

An alternative is to use a cheaper oil paint made by a reputable manufacturer. Rowney's 'Georgian' and Winsor and Newton's 'Winton' series are popular options, and many find there is little, if any, discernible difference between these and the artists' paints.

All oil paints are slow-drying, but some colours are faster than others. The earth pigments – including siennas, umbers and ochres – are usually the fastest-drying, with thin layers of paint drying in a day or two. Other colours, including alizarin crimson, may take ten days before the paint is dry to the touch. Complete drying can take up to a year. Because thick layers of paint dry slowly, it is best to build up your paint gradually in several thin coats.

Oil paints and oil pastels

The pigment also determines the stability and light-fastness, or permanence, of the colour. Most manufacturers have their own rating systems, which are printed on the tubes. Winsor and Newton, for instance, use AA for extremely permanent colours, A for durable, B for moderately durable and C for fugitive.

Painting 'fat over lean'

Traditionally, oil paints are applied 'fat over lean'. This means diluted, or 'lean', colour is used in the early stages, and the thicker textural colour is built up gradually as the painting progresses. 'Lean' paint is paint which has been diluted with turpentine, white spirit, oil of spike lavender or any other proprietary solvent.

'Fat' paint has been mixed with a traditional oil medium, such as linseed oil, safflower oil or poppy oil; or it may be mixed with one of the new alkyd-based media, such as Liquin or Oleopasto. There is more about painting media on pages 42–3.

When following the 'fat over lean' rule, it is important that the proportion of medium be increased with successive layers of paint if the layers of paint are to dry satisfactorily and create a physically stable painting.

Sticks of colour

Oil pastels and Oilbars are compatible with oil paints and many artists use them to introduce line and texture into their paintings. They are particularly useful for making the initial outline drawing prior to painting. The drawing can then be completely obliterated by successive layers of paint or, alternatively, the lines can be incorporated into the finished picture.

Oil pastels are comparatively hard but can be blended with turpentine applied with a brush or rag. Oilbars are actually oil paints in stick form and are more malleable.

PAINTING SURFACES

The simplest, quickest way of obtaining a 'support' – a painting surface – is to go to the art shop and buy a ready-stretched canvas or a specially prepared board. These come in a selection of sizes, and you can take one home and start work on it immediately. Surfaces are primed with an acrylic primer or with a glue size and oil primer. Both of these primed surfaces are suitable for use with oil paint.

Surface texture is an important consideration. Both boards and canvases come in a variety of grains. For small or detailed work, you may want a

Primed board

Canvas-covered board

Oil paper

fine texture; for larger works or if you like painting with thick paint, you may prefer a coarser surface. Most portrait painters use a fine surface, because it enables them to render essential detail more easily.

Ready-to-use canvases

For the beginner, artists' linen is probably the best, because it has an even texture and is ideal for detail. Artists' linen is made from flax and is the traditional quality surface for oil painting. It is light brown in colour and is available with a close, uniform weave or a slightly coarser weave.

For larger portraits, cotton duck, cream in colour, is less expensive than artists' linen and has a more open weave. Both cotton duck and artists' linen are available in a wide range of sizes from around 7 × 5 in (18 × 13 cm) to 48 × 36 in (122 × 91 cm).

Painting boards

Textured boards and canvas-covered boards are practical alternatives to stretched canvas. The canvas-covered boards come in varying textures and are literally pieces of primed canvas laminated on to rigid boards. They are lightweight, stable and easy to store. Painting boards have an imitation-canvas surface.

For quick colour sketches, oil-sketching paper is useful and is available with a fine, medium or coarse surface. You can buy it in pads or as individual sheets.

Making your own

There will be times when you want to make your own support, either because the bought varieties do not cater for the size or shape you require or because you want to try out a different texture, or to make a number of quick paintings, and ready-to-go surfaces work out too expensive. There are suggestions and instructions for making some of these on the following pages.

Stretched canvas

MAKING YOUR OWN SUPPORT

Many artists like to prepare their own supports. Not only does this give them complete control over what they paint on but the process itself can be satisfying and enjoyable. Whether you are stretching canvas, cutting board or priming paper, you will save time by making a number of supports in one session. And what better incentive to start work than a stack of newly prepared painting surfaces?

Stretching a canvas
You can buy and stretch your own canvas; it is available by the metre, unprimed or ready-primed, from any art shop. The main types of canvas are artists' linen and cotton duck. Jute is an inexpensive, though shorter-lived, alternative. Wooden stretcher sides are also available from art shops and these are simply slotted together at the corners.

Wood and board
Any wooden panel can be used with oils. The most popular are plywood and hardboard, and they have the advantage of being readily available and easy to cut to size. Large sheets may need batten supports on the back to help keep them rigid.

You might like to try making your own canvas-covered or muslin-covered board – easily done by sticking the fabric on one side of the board to give a

△ **2** *Staple the canvas to the back of the stretcher. Start by stapling the centre of each of the four sides, then work outwards towards the corners.*

rigid, textured surface. Muslin is much loved by artists who work on a small scale and find canvas bulky or coarse. It has a fine, crisp texture that is receptive to paint and also enhances the picture surface.

Card and paper
For quick colour sketches with oil paints, there is no reason why you should not use primed cardboard or even stiff paper. Many artists prefer working on disposable surfaces, finding it less inhibiting than painting on a prepared canvas or board. On a pristine support, it is easy to feel under pressure to produce a painting worthy of the surface, and the painting can be too tight as a result. Scraps of paper and cardboard, on the other hand, are disposable and therefore liberating.

These instant supports have another important

△ **1** *Slot together the wooden stretcher pieces, matching the bevelled edges. Cut canvas to fit, allowing a 1-in (2.5-cm) turnover at the back of the stretcher.*

△ **3** *Make an envelope of each corner, folding down first one edge, then the other.*

△ **4** *Secure the enveloped corners firmly with one or more staples.*

advantage. Purists may find this rather a cheat, but when working on paper or card you can change the composition at any time simply by cutting off unwanted support. If, for example, you feel there is too much empty space at the top of the portrait, you can get a ruler and scalpel and chop off the excess.

Preparation and priming

All supports used with oil paint must be primed. Whether you are using canvas, wood, card or paper, you need a primer to seal the porous surface. Not only does it provide a smooth surface, ready for the layers of colour, but it also helps preserve the support against the long-term effects of the paint. Canvas, for instance, will eventually start to rot if the oil paints are applied directly to unprimed fabric.

A few years ago, canvas, boards and other surfaces intended for oil painting were always sealed with glue size, and then given two or three coats of oil primer or some other oil-based foundation. Many artists still follow this traditional and well-tried method, but the oil primers require from one to three days' drying-time between coats, so the process is a long one.

Acrylic products provide quicker results and are quite suitable for use with oil paints. Two or three coats of acrylic gesso or acrylic-emulsion glaze will seal your painting surface. Acrylic matt medium dries transparently and can be used as a surface sealant if you want to retain the natural colour of the support.

△ **5** *Tap wooden corner-pieces into the reverse of the stretcher, making sure the canvas is loosely stretched but not taut.*

△ **6** *Prime with two coats of acrylic gesso, allowing the primer to dry between coats.*

THINNING AND THICKENING

Oil paint can be used directly from the tube, without diluting and without the addition of a medium to change or enhance its consistency. But paint on its own limits your work, and media are essential for most painting techniques, including the traditional 'fat over lean'.

Diluting the paints

A solvent is used for both diluting oil paint, which speeds up the drying-time, and cleaning brushes and palette after you have finished painting. The most popular solvent is turpentine, since it evaporates quickly, leaving no trace on the painted surface.

The best turpentine is pure and distilled, available from art shops. Turpentine substitute and white spirit are less expensive alternatives and can be bought at any decorating or hardware shop. Some artists feel these are inferior to the genuine article – certainly they do not smell as evocative and pleasant as genuine turpentine, which is made from the distilled resin of pine trees. A practical compromise is to use real turpentine with the paints and a cheaper substitute for cleaning up.

Traditional oils and media

A vegetable drying oil, or medium, is used to increase the gloss, transparency or texture of the colours – especially in the later stages of the painting, when the artist wants to create a lively, succulent paint surface after making a 'lean' start.

Oil paints are made by grinding pigment into a binder – a natural drying oil such as linseed, poppy or safflower. The oil binder gives the paint an even consistency and makes it easy to handle. Some of these binding oils are also used as paint media, linseed oil being the most widely employed.

You can also buy proprietary oil media – usually a combination of turpentine and either linseed or poppy oil. Different media fulfil different roles – improving the flow of the paint, creating transparent colour for glazing, enlivening the paint surface or producing a matt finish.

The modern option

Oil painting has changed dramatically in the last twenty years, thanks to a series of new media which have revolutionized painting techniques.

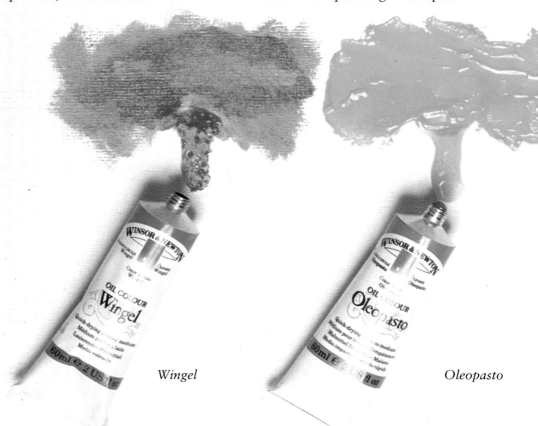

Wingel   *Oleopasto*

The new media are alkyds. These are not made from natural materials, such as oil and turpentine, but they are compatible with oils and considerably reduce the drying time of the paints.

Liquin is a viscous substance, used for thinning, for glazing and for depicting detail. Oleopasto is a texture paste, used for mixing with the paint in order to build up thick layers of colour that dry quickly without cracking. Wingel is an all-purpose medium, an alkyd version of the traditional oil-and-turpentine combination.

As with all new products, there are mixed feelings about alkyd media. Traditionalists feel they change the nature of oil painting; they do not like the tactile difference the media make to the paints. This difference is certainly enormous. Not only does the result look different but the paints actually feel different as you apply them.

Alkyd media, however, do have a large number of adherents. Two artists whose work is demonstrated on pages 74 and 84 are both comparatively recent converts to Liquin, but they now find it an essential part of their painting equipment.

▷ *The same subject, treated with the four different media, shows the range of effects that can be achieved.*

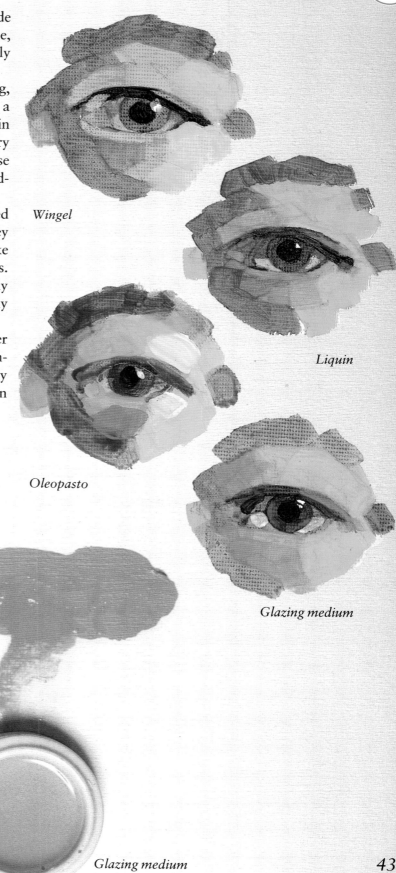

Wingel

Liquin

Oleopasto

Glazing medium

Liquin

Glazing medium

EASELS AND OTHER EQUIPMENT

The largest piece of equipment you are likely to need is an easel. A good easel will last a lifetime, so take a little time to find one that suits you. A standing easel is more practical for portraits than a sitting or table model, because you will occasionally want to be on a higher level than your sitter.

Portrait painting is usually done indoors, so portability is not a major consideration. But if you already have a lightweight, folding sketching easel, some models will take surprisingly large canvases – 54 in (137 cm) high and above, which is more than adequate for most portraits.

Studio easel

If you do want to invest in a more substantial model, solid studio easels will offer good service. They are so tough and long-lasting that they get handed down from generation to generation, and it is not unusual to find decent second-hand ones. Some studio easels fold for easier storage, but on the whole they are definitely not for moving around.

For a small or temporary studio, a radial easel is a good alternative. This all-round model is popular with art schools because it is both sturdy and practical. The three splayed feet can be adjusted or folded away, and the horizontal bar will hold brushes and pencils.

The palette

Depending on how you prefer to work, there are two basic types of palette. If you like to hold the palette in your hand as you paint, then the classical kidney-shaped or rectangular version with a thumb-hole is still the best. These come in various sizes and are made in wood or plastic. You can obtain disposal paper versions in pad form which are similarly shaped. These tear-off pads are a practical alternative.

Table easel

Sketching easel

Many artists, however, prefer to have their paints laid out on a stationary palette close by, so that they can keep both hands free to manipulate the paint. In this case, almost any wipeable material can be used for a palette, including wood, Perspex and glass. The height of the table on which the palette rests is important; it should be comfortable, so that you don't have to twist or bend to load the brush.

Other equipment
You now have the basic materials and equipment. Other items will accumulate alarmingly quickly as you need them. Jars and boxes are essential, for mixing and storage. A steady supply of clean rags is also useful. If you use a classical palette with a thumbhole, you may find you need clip-on dipper pots to hold turpentine, oil or other media.

Palette with clip-on dipper
containers for oil and turpentine

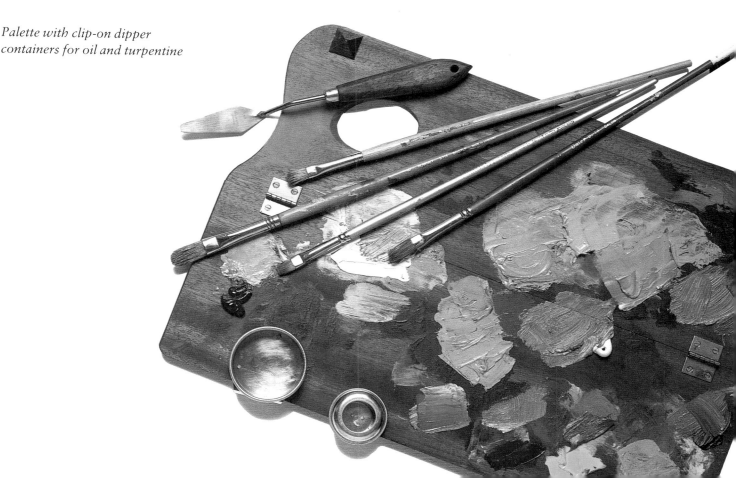

BRUSHES AND KNIVES

A Renaissance artist transported forward into the present century might feel surprisingly at home with modern brushes. The principles of brush-making have hardly changed over all those years, and key parts are still done by hand. Such an artist would also feel familiar with some of the materials used to make the more expensive brushes, although equally our time-traveller would be fascinated to examine some of the modern substitutes which mean many brushes are cheaper to buy.

A brush consists of the bristle or head, the ferrule (the metal neck holding the head in place) and the handle, which varies in length, although most oil-painting brushes are long, to enable the artist to stand back.

Brushes and knives for oil painting

Rounds, flats and filberts

All brushes worth using are quite expensive. Sound advice for the beginner is to buy one or two from the very top-quality range, made from a traditional material such as hog bristle, with ferrules of cupronickel or another good metal. But a lot of artists actually prefer the modern synthetic brushes. You could therefore explore these usually cheaper synthetic brushes to complete your initial collection of basic shapes.

ROUNDS are the most commonly used, with a circular ferrule and rounded, pointed head of bristles – the shape we instantly think of when we imagine a paintbrush. Versatile, they can be used

for large areas of colour as well as more delicate work.

FLATS have flattened, square heads to make short strokes and dab colour into textured areas. They can produce a stiffly 'impastoed', or thick, paint surface. The sides of flats can be used for painting thin lines.

BRIGHTS are shorter versions of flats and the heads are more rigid, giving what many regard as greater control.

FILBERTS look like 'rounded flats', tapered so that they become more of a general-purpose brush.

BLENDERS or **FANS** have flattened heads which are splayed out into a fan shape, so that they can blend two colours evenly.

DECORATOR'S BRUSHES are useful in the smaller sizes when working on a large scale, for blocking in areas of colour.

Sizes of brushes are indicated by numbers on the handles, but a No. 10 made by one manufacturer might differ in length from a No. 10 made by someone else.

Do's and don'ts
DO look after your brushes and you will then find that the more expensive ones last for many years. Clean them with white spirit or turpentine, and soap and cold water, at the end of each painting session.

DO allow brushes to dry naturally, with bristles upwards.

DON'T stand brushes on their bristles in the turpentine or spirit while you are painting, or they will lose their shape.

Knives
A painting knife has a cranked, or bent, handle rather like a trowel. It is used for applying thick, 'impastoed' paint.

A palette knife has a straight handle. It is used for mixing colour and scraping the palette clean.

Both types of knife come in a variety of shapes and sizes.

CHAPTER (5) CHAPTER

Portrait projects

THIS SECTION of the book is purely practical. It covers techniques and methods which are particularly appropriate to portraiture, and demonstrates how these are applied in an actual painting. We asked a number of artists to make a contribution. Each has brought his or her own ways of working, and each employs different techniques and principles. The artists also chose different materials and worked from their own choice of palette.

Ian Sidaway works systematically and accurately, often enlarging a precise preliminary drawing on to the canvas using a grid system. Both the technique and its application are clearly shown in his portrait of a young girl. Suzanne O'Riley, on the other hand, works more intuitively. She often makes small colour sketches, but these are more for exploratory reasons than as a specific stage towards the final product. These are two of the diverse approaches employed by the artists.

You are advised to use these projects as guidelines for work of your own choice – with your own subjects. The projects illustrated here are for you to enjoy and learn from.

Suzanne O'Riley painted
this portrait of Doug
Hayward with soft brush-
strokes and undefined
patches of colour. Seen
from close-quarters, the
image is hazy and blurred.
Looked at as a whole, the
softly laid colour describes
a solid, structured figure.

TECHNIQUES

COLOUR SKETCHES

Tiny colour sketches are a good starting point for a portrait. They allow you to see at a glance how the finished portrait will look, and whether it is worth pursuing a particular pose.

These pocket-sized sketchbook colour notes were made by artist Suzanne O'Riley, who painted the portrait on the following pages. Suzanne usually starts with a sketchbook miniature, saying it gives her a feel for the subject. She is not interested in detail at this early stage, and often paints these miniatures with a very large brush.

The sketches were done in oil, with the palette that Suzanne will eventually use for the actual portrait. She likes to do them spontaneously, without having to think ahead and prepare her surface. She also likes to use the same colours and materials that she will eventually use in the finished portrait.

As well as being a useful first step towards a larger painting, these tiny preliminary sketches are delightful in their own right. Some of the sketches shown here were developed later as larger portraits. The artist was able to see from each sketch whether the lighting, colours, tones and composition were workable, and whether or not they would translate effectively on to a larger scale.

Tiny colour sketches made in a pocket-sized sketchbook by Suzanne O'Riley. The artist often makes these quick oil sketches before starting on a larger work of the same subject.

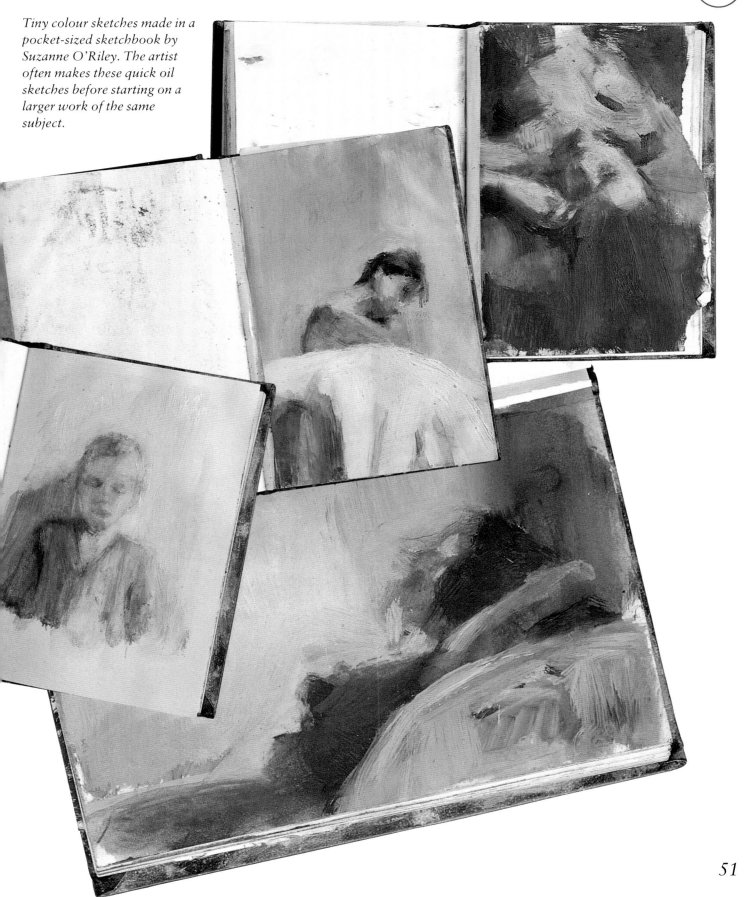

TECHNIQUES

PRELIMINARY DRAWINGS

The practice of making a preliminary drawing prior to starting a painting is a usual one, especially with portrait artists. The human face is a complicated structure; it takes time to become familiar with the features, expressions and other component parts.

And there is another reason for a preliminary drawing. It is quite common to hear portrait artists say they like painting subjects they know well. Unfortunately, with professional portrait artists at least, the majority of sitters are total strangers. Not only does the artist have to become acquainted with a new face but he or she often has to produce a portrait that fits in with the sitter's self-image. Frequently, portraits which are actually perfect likenesses are rejected by sitters simply because they do not portray the subjects as those subjects see themselves.

A preliminary drawing therefore serves two purposes. First, it helps the artist to get to know a face before painting it. Second, it tells the sitter what to expect. The preliminary drawing can be shown to the sitter, who can, at this early stage, say whether this is how he or she wants to be portrayed in the final painting.

Why charcoal?

Suzanne O'Riley used charcoal for this preliminary drawing before going on to do the painting on the next page. Charcoal is one of her favourite media, both for quick sketches and for more finished

△ *The artist looks at the model in various poses and makes drawings to help her decide on a final composition. After trying various angles, the sitter is positioned facing the direct light of a window.*

▷ *The first trial drawing shows the model in profile. The artist uses charcoal on paper, rubbing back to the white paper with a kneadable eraser to create highlights.*

drawings. Some of her large charcoal drawings take two or three days. This sketch was done very quickly, the object being to get down a lot of information in a short time.

If you are not used to making preliminary drawings, charcoal is an ideal medium. Not only can you work quickly but you can also rub out and change things easily while still keeping the drawing lively and fluid. As you can see from these pictures, Suzanne O'Riley uses the side of the charcoal stick to block in large areas of tone. She then rubs back into the charcoal, 'drawing' with an eraser to create highlights and light tones.

Broad and chunky, charcoal is good for the novice because it is too clumsy to be used for detail. Thus the temptation to overwork a drawing or to make it too tight ceases to be a problem. Charcoal comes in various sizes: the large sticks are very chunky and used mostly by stage designers for drawing up backcloths.

The other great advantage of charcoal is that you can work on a large scale. You can, if you wish, make your drawing as big as the proposed painting. If you are happy with your drawing, it can be transferred easily on to the support without enlarging or making any scale adjustment.

△ *A drawing showing a three-quarters view of the model, also done in charcoal. Here the artist blocks in areas of tone using the side of the stick.*

◁ *To acquaint herself further with the model, the artist makes a charcoal sketch in a pocket-sized sketchbook.*

◁ *A small sketchbook study done in oils. The same colours will eventually be used in the larger painting.*

PROJECTS

PORTRAIT OF LESLEY

The most striking aspect of this portrait is that everything is painted in very general terms. Yet, as a whole, the portrait works beautifully. The eyes are observed and painted in exactly the same way as the rest of the subject, with no pupils, highlights or any of the other details which we 'know' are there. Suzanne O'Riley paints exactly what she sees – broad strokes of tone which, from close-quarters, are unrecognizable blobs.

As in all of her paintings, the lighting here is important. The subject is lit by natural daylight from the window at one side. This softens the far side of the face, which appears to merge with the blue of the background – some of the flesh colours being tonally very similar to the cool blue of the wall. In the finished painting there is no visible defining contour line between face and background.

Flesh tones

The planes of light and dark, warm and cool, are closely observed and established but painted as soft strokes of colour, not harshly defined shapes.

This is partly because the artist uses the technique of looking at the subject through half-closed eyes. The resulting hazy view obscures much of the local colour and enables her to see clearly the areas of light and shade which describe the form. Also, she paints these with large brushes, moving to and fro, relating one tone to its neighbour and obliterating detail until she is satisfied with the result.

Suzanne O'Riley says she always spends time observing and then 'allows the hand to react to the eye'. She often paints while gazing at the sitter, not looking at the painting for quite a few seconds. 'You must look for form,' she says. 'Forget you are painting a nose or eye, just concentrate on what you can see. And above all, don't worry about the likeness. That will come if everything else works.'

△ **1** *After making a number of preliminary sketches, the artist decides on a three-quarters view for the portrait, with the model sitting in front of a plain blue wall.*

◁ **3** *Working on a tinted canvas, the artist paints an outline in Payne's grey and Prussian blue – 'always a light outline because it is easier to correct'. She starts to lay the background in Prussian blue and white.*

▽ **4** *The background colour is taken up to the head with a large brush. Bold strokes are used to redraw the contours of the head with background colour.*

◁ **2** *The artist says her palette tends to change according to mood. Colours in this portrait include Payne's grey, Prussian blue, Naples yellow, burnt sienna, raw umber, yellow ochre, cadmium red deep, flesh tint and terre-verte. She never uses black.*

55

▽ 5 *Light and dark sweater colours are painted in mixtures of viridian and white. For the face, the artist works across the image, using three or four different brushes to block in patches of light and dark in approximate tones. Flesh tones are painted in mixtures which include yellow ochre, flesh tint, Naples yellow and 'a lot of blue'. The artist deliberately uses big brushes, forcing herself to concentrate on general areas rather than detail.*

▷ 6 *The main tones and colours are now established. The artist works quickly to develop the whole picture instead of concentrating on particular areas.*

△ 7 The hair is treated in exactly the same way as the face, background and sweater – in loose strokes of tone. Here, the artist paints a broad plane of highlight into the hair.

△ 8 Still working with a large brush, the artist develops the flesh tones. As before, the strokes are broad and general. 'I paint what I see, not what I know to be there,' she explains. 'My hand always reacts to my eye.'

▽ 9 Overlaid strokes of light and dark flesh tones are built up. Gradually, the underlying facial forms emerge – the result of closely observed planes of light and shade.

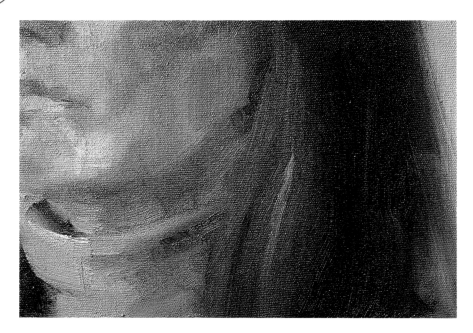

◁ **10** *A close-up of the skin and hair shows only subtle differences between the patches of colour. There are no stark tonal contrasts and no linear brushstrokes. The hair is painted in mixtures of burnt sienna, viridian, Naples yellow and 'lots of blue'.*

▽ **11** *Eyes are kept very general. The artist has established them as patches of loose tone, with no highlights and no deep shadows. The pupils were not visible and were therefore not painted.*

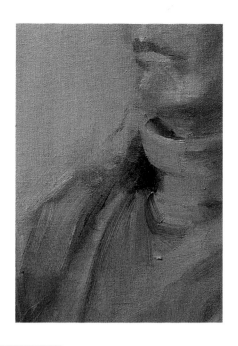

◁ **12** *The sweater is sketchily painted in light and dark mixtures of viridian and white, toned down with colours used elsewhere in the picture.*

▷ **13** *Despite being painted against a flat background, the artist has created a sense of space and perspective by allowing the model's face to recede into the background. The face has no defining line and the cool flesh tones furthest away from the artist merge into the blue of the background wall.*

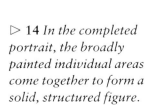

▷ **14** *In the completed portrait, the broadly painted individual areas come together to form a solid, structured figure.*

TECHNIQUES

FROM DRAWING TO PAINTING

We have seen that many painters start work with preliminary studies. These may take the form of tiny sketches, detailed drawings, colour studies and so on. The approach varies, but the purpose is the same – to find out as much as possible before committing paint to canvas.

Sketches and preliminary drawings are usually fresh and spontaneous. The artist is not afraid to use loose, scribbly strokes because it does not matter how the drawing will 'look'.

Enlarging the drawing
When you have made a sketch or drawing which satisfies you, it is a simple matter to enlarge and transfer this on to the canvas so that it is ready to paint. The secret is to transfer the image without losing the freshness of the original sketch.

First, divide the canvas or painting surface into a number of equal squares or rectangles using pencil and ruler. Next, draw a grid over the drawing, making the same number of squares or rectangles of the same proportion as those on the canvas. Now –

the tricky part – transfer the image a square at a time on to the canvas.

Keep the drawing loose and fluid. Avoid making the new image too small or cramped. If you feel this is happening, switch to charcoal so that the new drawing is chunky and bold. Try drawing from the shoulder or elbow rather than from the wrist. This way, the drawing will be more fluid and free. It is not necessary to transfer every detail from the small drawing. Sometimes the merest outline is a sufficient guide for the paint, and you can always refer back to the original small drawing as you paint.

Working from photographs
Photographs are often a useful additional reference, especially for details. The camera records a split second and you can use this as a means of establishing folds in clothing, the way the hair falls and other changing or unstable elements.

Most painters, however, do not work solely from a photograph. A camera is unselective and tends to make the subject look flatter and less interesting than it really is. The human eye works in reverse, selecting and emphasizing those elements which make the portrait interesting.

This may sound like old-fashioned teaching and you may not be convinced until you have actually tried to work from a photograph. When you do, you will find it surprisingly difficult to get tonal contrast, depth and life into your picture unless you have drawings or some other form of reference to back this up.

Many portrait painters take extensive photographs of the sitter, as well as making a number of drawings. These can be referred to in between sittings, when the model is not available, but they will rarely suffice for long as a substitute for the sitter.

LINEX A 34
ACRYL
DENMARK

▽ **1** *The artist intends to use this watercolour study as the basis for a larger oil painting. To draw the image accurately on to the larger canvas, he first measures and divides the study into a grid of squares.*

△ 2 *The canvas is then divided into the same number of squares. Now, the artist draws the image on to the canvas, copying a square at a time from the smaller watercolour on to the large canvas.*

△ **3** *The image on the small watercolour is transferred to the large canvas ready for painting. You can use charcoal, oil pastel or paint as an alternative for the large-scale drawing.*

PROJECTS

YOUNG GIRL

This is the only portrait in the book that was not painted directly from the model. The artist, Ian Sidaway, likes working from detailed references – here a photograph and this watercolour sketch.

Preliminary studies

Ian Sidaway trained as an illustrator and his paintings have a precision and graphic quality which reflect this period in his life. He is not an artist who makes rough preliminary sketches. His preliminaries are detailed drawings and water-colours – complete works in their own right. He finds them useful to show clients prior to starting on the final painting because they are a good indication of how the finished portrait will look.

The watercolour here was used to work out the balance of tones within the composition. By the time he started the oil painting, the artist knew exactly where the planes of light and shade fell on the girl's face. He had also worked out the tonal arrangement, and knew which parts of the figure would be light or dark in relation to the background.

Patches of colour

Ian Sidaway's approach to painting is not the traditional one of developing the whole image simultaneously. Although he does go back over his work, adjusting colours and tones, his approach generally is a systematic one. He draws in detail exactly where each plane of light, each patch of colour, will be. Then he starts to paint, moving from one precisely drawn patch to another. Each new tone and colour is related to its immediate neighbours as he works across the canvas.

Unusually, Ian Sidaway does not feel it necessary to get rid of the white canvas before being able to assess colours and tones. Although certain areas are modified as is thought necessary, each tone and colour is essentially right in relation to the image as a whole. The technique looks effortless, but it actually calls for a practised eye and a lot of planning.

△ **1** *Before starting the portrait in oils, the artist first took reference photographs of the subject and made this watercolour sketch.*

▷ **3** *For the mid-tones of the hair, the artist adds a little yellow ochre, chromium orange and titanium white to the first mixture.*

▽ **4** *The lightest hair tone is obtained by adding more white to the previous colour.*

◁ **2** *Beginning with the dark tones, the artist blocks in facial shadows and some dark hair tones with a mixture of French ultramarine and raw umber. Other dark hair tones have added cadmium red and yellow ochre.*

63

△ **5** *For the dark and mid-tones of the face, the artist modifies the light hair mixture by adding cobalt blue, cadmium red and titanium white.*

▷ **6** *Hair and flesh tones are painted in the same basic colours. By changing and modifying the basic mixtures in this way, a harmony of colour and tone is achieved throughout the whole image.*

64

◁ 7 *White is added to the existing facial mix in varying proportions for the pale skin tones.*

▽ 8 *The girl's shirt is blocked in with black. Here the artist paints the lighter areas in grey.*

△ **9** *Using a mixture of sap green and lemon yellow, the artist starts to paint the background foliage in short, loose brush-strokes.*

◁ **10** *The background is now complete. The background green is taken up to and around the figure, cutting crisply into the hair and shirt in order to clarify and redefine the shapes.*

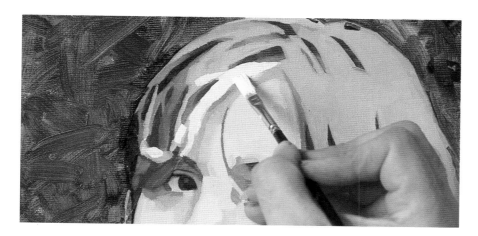

◁ **11** *Finally, the highlights of the hair are painted, with the lightest hair tone mixed with titanium white.*

▽ **12** *The artist used just nine colours for this portrait: raw umber, cadmium red, French ultramarine, yellow ochre, titanium white, chrome orange, cobalt blue, sap green and lemon yellow.*

TECHNIQUES

DRAWING IN OIL

You might find it easier to make the initial outline drawing in oil pastel or Oilbar rather than in paint. This simplifies the early stages of the painting and means you can concentrate entirely on the drawing, without having to worry about mixing paint and choosing brushes. Both materials are completely compatible with oil paint. The initial drawing can be covered up as the picture progresses, or the lines emphasized and used in the painting.

Martin Stamford is not a purist when it comes to oil painting, and he is quite happy to introduce other elements into the picture if he feels this will create interest or produce a livelier image. Because he mixed Liquin with the paint in the earlier stages, the paint dried relatively quickly and he was soon able to use both oil pastel and Oilbar on top of the dry colour. In his painting on pages 74–81, he redrew the fabric folds and added highlights to complete the picture.

Oilbars

Oil paint has no equivalent, but it has a rival. The new Oilbars are paints in stick form. They can be used instead of paint and many oil-painting techniques can be achieved equally well with the painting sticks. They can also be used with oil paints and oil pastels – as the artist Martin Stamford does in his demonstration portrait.

The sticks come in three sizes – the smaller ones are good for linear drawing; the largest are very chunky and suitable for large-scale work. Before using a stick of Oilbar, you must remove the waxy sealant that keeps the colour soft. The sealant re-forms to protect the stick, so it must be removed each time you start work.

Oil pastels

Oil pastels are long-time favourites for strong colour effects and for quick sketches. They are very much a medium in their own right and as such do not really have a place in a book on oil painting. However, many artists use oil pastels and oil paints together in the same work and, for this reason, it is useful to look at some of the effects which can be achieved.

Although colours can be dissolved and blended with turpentine once they are on the canvas, oil pastels are not a subtle medium and it is not easy to obtain close tonal effects. Their strength lies in their boldness and immediacy and it is in this capacity that most artists use them.

The nice thing about both oil pastels and Oilbars is that there need be no colour-mixing prior to painting. Oilbars are much softer than pastels and they can be mixed. Oil pastels are quite hard and are difficult to blend unless you dissolve the colours with turps. But as linear media, complementary to the paint, they are both superb.

Line drawing in oil pastel and Oilbars *The finer lines are made with oil pastel, using the sharper edge of the end of the stick. Oilbar is used for broader, softer lines.*

PROJECTS

EXPLORING MEDIA

There are no rules about what to use for your working drawings. Draw with any medium you like and feel free to experiment with different combinations. The only restrictions are those which come from the materials themselves, because certain things do not mix. Oil-based materials will not work with water-based ones, for instance. But even here, oil and water create interesting effects when they resist and run off each other. Basically, then, you can draw with anything that makes a mark.

Before embarking on any drawing, whether it is a preliminary sketch for your portrait, a thumbnail sketch or a more finished drawing, consider your options. Different materials bring out different aspects of what you are drawing. You can choose from pencil, charcoal, technical pen, ballpoint pen, dip pen and ink, coloured pencil, pastel, crayon and many more.

Three approaches
The same model sits in three poses. In each the lighting is changed and she is wearing different clothes. Before starting to paint, artist Martin Stamford was anxious to exploit the qualities of each pose and to draw it in a new way, using different materials, each chosen to capture the special qualities of the pose.

The first pose is one of contrasting tones and strong light; there is very little colour. The artist chose white paper and chunky charcoal to capture the emphatic lights and darks of the subject. He then used a kneadable eraser to rub back into the dark tones, creating highlights on the hair and face.

The second pose is more subtle, with very little colour, but a perforated straw hat causes flecks of light to fall across the model's face. The tiny shapes of speckled light call for a more detailed approach and for this the artist chose graphite pencil.

△ ▷ **Charcoal** *Because the subject is mainly black and white, the artist finds chunky charcoal ideal for blocking in the broad areas of contrasting tone.*

In the most colourful pose, the sitter wears a bright turquoise shirt and poses against a white wall. The light falls on the figure from two points – the windows on each side of the model. The fluid lines of the shirt are important here and the artist used a combination of pencil and oil pastel – the pastels to block in areas of bold colour, the pencil to define the sweeps of fabric and a minimum amount of tone.

△ ▷ **Pencil** *Fine lines are made with the sharpened point of a hard (H) graphite pencil; areas of shadow are blocked in with the edge of a softer (4B) point.*

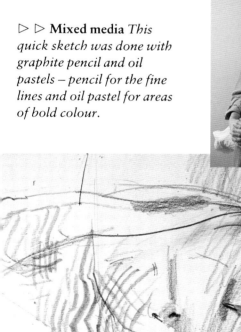

▷ ▷ **Mixed media** *This quick sketch was done with graphite pencil and oil pastels – pencil for the fine lines and oil pastel for areas of bold colour.*

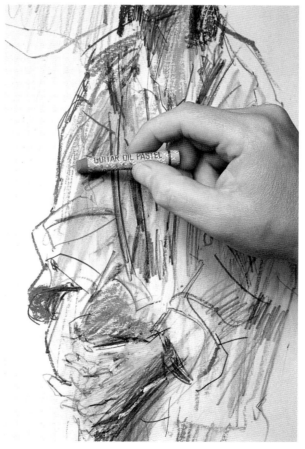

When we asked Martin Stamford to do the demonstration painting on the following pages, he started by making these drawings. The main objective was to find the right pose and composition, so the model was asked to wear different clothes and colours for each pose.

Each pose has certain qualities, and the artist chose his materials accordingly: charcoal on white paper for the tonal sketch; pencil to convey the line and dappled light of the sun hat; oil pastel for colourful drapery.

73

PROJECTS

PORTRAIT IN PROFILE

This mixed-media picture was done in oil paints, oil pastels and Oilbars. Artist Martin Stamford is a great advocate of Liquin and used this with the paint, which then dried quickly enough for the pastels and Oilbars to be used on top. The combination of colour and texture turns a formal pose into an unusual and lively portrait.

Before starting, Stamford spent a lot of time deciding on the pose. The drawings on the preceding pages were part of the decision-making process. His great concern was lighting. The sitter is between two windows, which produced equally strong light on her front and back, making the subject look too symmetrical. After trying several different poses, he decided upon a profile with strong frontal light. The second window, behind the sitter, was covered with a white sheet to soften the effect.

Don't forget the corners!
When planning the painting, the artist was careful not to make the composition too symmetrical. The subject was therefore placed slightly to one side of the canvas, while the shapes of the surrounding background were also taken into consideration. The background shapes are positive and make a contribution to the painting as a whole. There is no superfluous empty space around the subject.

When painting portraits on a rectangular support, it is easy to forget the corners and merely fill them in with background colour. Martin Stamford says he is always conscious of this common oversight. His advice is to use the whole rectangle to make sure the shapes formed by the background are as strong as those formed by the subject itself.

Classical beginnings
In the early stages, the portrait is painted in a classical manner, with the initial drawing being done in diluted blue paint. From this point onwards, tone and colour are applied across the entire image. No part of the painting is brought to a finished state because Stamford likes to keep the whole piece in a state of flux for as long as possible.

'I create an image in order to develop it, not to finish it,' he explains. 'The painting will tell me when it is finished. As it is, I always paint for tomorrow.'

△ **1** *After making several exploratory sketches, the model is seated in profile looking towards the window.*

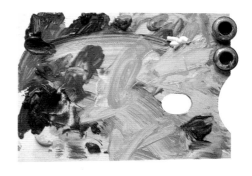

△ **2** *During the initial stages, the palette includes white, yellow ochre, cerulean blue, light red, raw umber, monestial turquoise, cerulean blue, black, cadmium yellow and terre-verte.*

▷ **3** *Working on primed hardboard, the artist paints an outline in a very diluted wash of blue and black.*

▽ **4** *Colour goes in early – flesh tones are yellow ochre, light red and raw umber, mixed with a very little white – 'just enough to reduce the colours without turning them chalky'.*

▷ **5** *Main colour areas are established. The hair is raw umber; the shirt, light and dark mixtures of cerulean, raw umber, monestial turquoise and white.*

◁ **6** *Facial tones have been developed and the background is painted with a small decorator's brush.*

▽ **7** *The artist stresses that brush-strokes should not follow the form of the subject – especially the curved and rounded forms of the human figure and face. His own strokes cut across the form in strong directional planes.*

◁ **8** *The artist works into the flesh colour, establishing carefully observed patches of cool shadow. These are made by mixing basic skin colours with blue.*

△ **9** *The folds of clothing are developed and emphasized. Here, highlights on the shirt are painted in thickly impastoed pale blue applied with a large brush.*

▽ **11** *Feeling the paint is too thick in places, the artist removes excess colour with a tissue. Again, he stresses the importance of keeping the painting flexible and 'on the move'.*

△ **10** *Colours and tones are now in place. The whole image is developed evenly as the artist follows his own advice: 'Never finish one part or focus on a particular area. Keep it all general.'*

79

△ **12** *In certain parts of the portrait, the paint has been wiped back almost to the primed board, leaving those areas thin enough to be reworked.*

▽ **13** *Liquin and turpentine speed up the drying-time of the paint. The artist is now able to develop the paint with Oilbar and oil pastels by introducing bright flecks of colour.*

△ **14** *White Oilbar establishes and defines highlights. The artist feels the narrow area of white T-shirt is important to the composition because it divides the shirt into two positive shapes.*

▷ **15** *The finished painting retains the vigour of the early stages. The secret, says the artist, is to make every shape alive and interesting – especially the shapes of empty background.*

TECHNIQUES

GLAZING AND IMPASTO

Two of the most used painting techniques are glazing and impasto. Glazing is the name given to overlaid transparent layers of thin paint in which the underlying colours glow through the glazed colour. Impasto paint is built up in thick layers, either with a brush or with a knife. Sometimes the two techniques are combined and we find transparent glazes over thickly impastoed paint.

Glazing

A glaze is a layer of transparent colour applied over a primed ground, an underpainting, another glaze or an impasto surface. Light passes through the glazed colour and is reflected back by the opaque undercolour. The undercolour must be completely dry before a glaze can be applied. When several glazes are applied in this way, the effect is quite different from those achieved with opaque painting.

Artists from the Renaissance onwards have used glazes, often combining these with other techniques and often using glazes only in certain parts of the painting, particularly on flesh tones.

Portrait painters through the ages have relied on glazing to capture the translucent quality of skin.

We often look at a subject and find an area of flesh that defies mixing – skin tone that is neither warm nor cool but an indefinable mixture of both. No single opaque colour will capture this effect, but a warm colour glazed over a cooler one will often get very close.

△ 1 *For a thickly impastoed effect, the artist mixes oil paint with Oleopasto.*

△ 2 *The thickened colour is laid with a painting knife.*

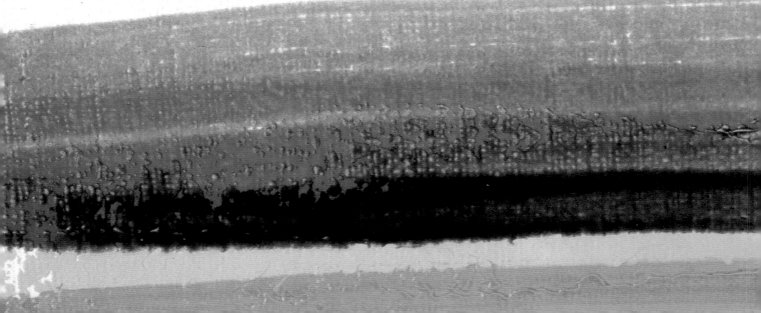

The oil painting technique known as 'grisaille' involves starting a picture with a monochrome underpainting in black, white and various tones of grey. The purpose of this is to allow the artist to establish the tones of a painting before introducing colour. Colour is usually applied in the form of glazes over the black and white.

Some pigments are well suited to glazing. Others are naturally opaque, making it difficult to get a truly transparent effect. Traditional glazes were mixed with various media of oil, varnish and turpentine. Today, modern glazing media, including the alkyd-based Liquin, make glazing a less complicated process.

Turpentine on its own should never be used as a glazing medium because, although it will dilute the colour, it will dry with a dull, opaque finish that has none of the reflective qualities of a real glaze.

Impasto

The slow-drying nature of oils has always been a restricting factor when using impasto techniques. Very thick wedges of paint take a long time to dry and have a tendency to crack. The practical alternative is to build up colour in layers, but this is also a long process, because each layer has to dry before the next can be applied.

However, new products have made impasto a much more practical proposition. Fast-drying texture pastes can be mixed with the paint when thick layers of colour are needed.

With the impasto technique, raised brush- and knife-strokes remain visible on the painted surface. These can be incorporated into the image, producing swirls of colour, stipples and many other effects. A painting knife enables you to lay broad areas of flat paint or apply paint in overlapping wedges.

△ 3 *A thin glaze is created by mixing oil paint with glazing medium.*

△ 4 *The transparent glaze is applied over the dry impastoed colour.*

PROJECTS

THE ARTIST'S FATHER

The painter of this and the next portrait is Humphrey Bangham; the sitter is the artist's father. The artist has painted this face several times before and is familiar with every aspect of it. For the purpose of these paintings, the familiarity was a bonus because the artist was free to concentrate on the techniques and work in hand without having to spend time getting to know a new face.

The artist prefers to start work with the paint, so there were no sketches or preliminary drawings for this painting. However, he took trouble to arrange the pose and lighting. He also spent time looking at and planning the composition before starting to paint.

A classical start

The initial painted drawing is done in raw umber – a traditional beginning. The paint is diluted with turpentine and mixed with Liquin. Humphrey Bangham says he now uses Liquin in most of his work. He likes the flowing consistency it gives to the paint. He also finds that it dries to a 'tacky' finish quite quickly, providing the best surface on which to scumble, or achieve broken colour.

When not working on a tinted board, the artist likes to obliterate the primed white canvas as quickly as possible, because he finds this interferes with ensuing tones and colours. This he does with diluted raw umber and white, with touches of ultramarine for the cooler tones. The result is a near-monochrome underpainting – a classical beginning when painting in oil.

Flesh tones

Once the tones of the picture have been established, the artist prefers to use little or no white. He finds that white makes the colours look chalky, and the paints dry more quickly without white.

The artist paints the planes of light and shade in broad sweeps, keeping the whole image alive and in a state of flux. As the image develops, he says, the colours and tones become stronger. Very pale tones on the features show the direction of light across the head; the light source thus defines the form.

△ *The sitter is made comfortable, while the artist considers how he will approach his new study.*

△ **1** *There is a strong directional light here, leaving one side of the model's face in the shade.*

△ **2** *The palette includes burnt umber, burnt sienna, yellow ochre, raw sienna, French ultramarine, Indian red, cadmium yellow, vermilion and geranium lake.*

△ **3** *For the initial outline drawing, the artist mixes raw umber with enough Liquin to thin the colour and give the paint a smooth flow.*

◁ **4** *The artist feels an accurate and structured drawing is essential for this type of painting. He constantly checks the position and proportions of the subject in relation to surrounding vertical and horizontal elements.*

85

△ 5 *To get rid of distracting white canvas, the main areas of tone are quickly washed in with umber and grey.*

▷ 6 *Flesh tones are painted as broad strokes of warm and cool colour. Humphrey Bangham prefers to start with the cooler tones – mixed mainly from white, raw umber and ultramarine.*

▷ ▷ 7 *Background tones are strengthened. The artist takes the background colour up to and around the subject, redefining the contours of the head and face. Here the artist uses a fine brush to clarify internal facial contours.*

86

▷ **8** *The artist builds up the planes of flesh, introducing warm and light tones into the cooler underpainting. The new tones are mixed mainly from vermilion, cadmium yellow, yellow ochre, burnt umber and burnt sienna.*

◁ **9** *The face is made up of broad planes of light and shade, loosely painted in warm and cool tones. By looking at the subject through half-closed eyes, the artist was able to pick out these planes more easily.*

▷ **10** *Finally, the background is completed, simplified into blocks of tone and colour.*

PROJECTS

PORTRAIT 'ALLA PRIMA'

When he is not painting, Humphrey Bangham designs and creates film-sets. The skill and versatility needed for this give him a flexibility that many painters do not have. The result is a wide repertoire of techniques and an enviable ability to create different effects and work in a variety of ways.

His first painting on pages 84–9 shows a classical approach to portraiture in oils. His second painting, illustrated here, demonstrates a very different approach. The palette is the same, but here there is no preliminary outline, no monochrome underpainting. Instead, the artist starts straight away by blocking in the main shapes and colours of the subject on a tinted canvas.

Alla prima

Taken literally, 'alla prima' means painted at one go or at one sitting. More generally, it describes the direct approach demonstrated in this painting.

Although no actual outline drawing was made prior to painting, the artist argues that the initial blocking in of principal shapes is in itself a type of drawing, albeit one which concentrates on volume rather than outline. He points out that the shapes are placed in relationship to each other; corrections are made by adjusting or moving those shapes; the background is painted up to and around the figure and, in effect, defines and 'redraws' the subject.

Humphrey Bangham works quickly, keeping the image fresh with a broad, general approach and constant reappraisal of the painting. Most of the time he uses large brushes, preferably stiff hog's-hair ones, occasionally switching to a finer sable brush for certain detail and 'key' line drawing.

Watching him work, it is noticeable how often he looks at the subject, his eyes moving almost constantly from sitter to canvas and back again. He frequently paints while looking at the subject rather than the canvas. Occasionally he looks at the subject through partially closed eyes in order to cut out some of the local colour and much of the distracting detail. This way, he says, you can see where the overall image is going wrong.

△ **1** *For this portrait, the model wears a pale shirt and sits against a blue background.*

△ **2** *The palette is the same as for the previous portrait, with the addition of cadmium orange, manganese blue and emerald green. The artist also uses turpentine and Liquin.*

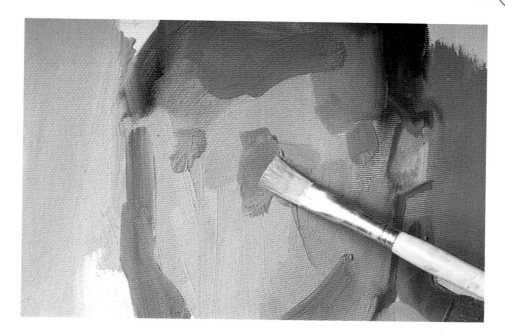

▷ **3** *The artist starts by blocking in areas of colour, starting with the background and broad flesh tones.*

◁ **4** *Painting is kept general so that changes can be made. The shirt is painted in mixtures of emerald green, manganese blue and a lot of white.*

91

◁ 5 *Still working in broad terms with a large brush, the cool flesh tones are mixed mainly from raw umber and white.*

▷ 6 *Colour relationships are so far accurately established without detail and without the help of a linear drawing.*

◁ 7 *The face is further developed in broad planes of warm and cool colour.*

△ 8 *Care is taken not to overemphasize the eyes, established as flat areas of tonally relating mid-brown.*

93

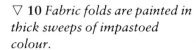

◁ **9** *Working across the image as a whole, the artist introduces brighter colours, emphasizing the contrast between planes of light and shadow. Highlights and shadows are thus strengthened.*

▽ **10** *Fabric folds are painted in thick sweeps of impastoed colour.*

▷ **11** *The shirt is painted in three or four tones of blue. Each tone is loosely established as a flat shape.*

▷ **12** *The completed picture is an arrangement of related tone and colour. 'To me the internal relationships are more important than being totally faithful to the subject. The result may be lighter or darker than the subject, but the overall tones should work in relationship to each other.'*

INDEX